CAMELOT

LERNER • LOEWE

STAGE VERSION

Opening Date: December 3, 1960
First Run: 873 performances
Location: Majestic Theatre, New York
Book: Alan Jay Lerner (based on *The Once and Future King* by T. H. White)
Director: Moss Hart
Original Cast Members: Richard Burton (King Arthur), Julie Andrews (Queen Guenevere), Robert Goulet (Sir Lancelot), and Roddy MacDowall (Mordred)
Standout Songs: "Camelot," "If Ever I Would Leave You," "I Loved You Once in Silence," "How to Handle a Woman."
Awards: The original production won four Tony Awards®, including Best Actor (Richard Burton).
Trivia: Both Richard Burton and Robert Goulet made their Broadway musical debuts in the show. *Camelot* was a favorite of President-elect John F. Kennedy, a fact that helped romanticize his administration, linking it with the show, and bestowing upon the Kennedys an aura of royalty that continues to this day. Lyricist Alan Jay Lerner and Kennedy were classmates at Harvard University.

FILM VERSION

Release Date: October 25, 1967
Director: Joshua Logan
Cast Members: Richard Harris (King Arthur), Vanessa Redgrave (Queen Guenevere), Franco Nero (Sir Lancelot), and David Hemmings (Mordred). Nero's vocals were dubbed by Gene Merlino.
Awards: The film won three Oscars®, for Best Art Direction, Costume Design, and Music Scoring.
Trivia: Warner Brothers studio head Jack L. Warner wanted Burton and Andrews to reprise their stage roles in the movie version, but each turned down the offer. Director Joshua Logan's first choices, Harris and Redgrave, were eventually given the parts. Two medieval castles in Spain were used as sets in the film as well as a specially built structure in Warner Brothers' back lot. This latter set was later used in the television series *Kung Fu*. In December 2006, nearly four decades after the film's release, co-stars Vanessa Redgrave and Franco Nero were married.

Alfred Publishing Co., Inc.
16320 Roscoe Blvd., Suite 100
P.O. Box 10003
Van Nuys, CA 91410-0003
alfred.com

ISBN-10: 0-7390-5489-9
ISBN-13: 978-0-7390-5489-5

CAMELOT

LERNER • LOEWE

FOREWORD

After the phenomenal success of *My Fair Lady* (item 27660 in Alfred's "Classic Musical Editions" series), playwright and lyricist Alan Jay Lerner was faced with a daunting task when deciding on a property for his next Broadway musical. Ultimately, Lerner and director Moss Hart chose to adapt T. H. White's novel *The Once and Future King*, which concerns the medieval British ruler King Arthur, his queen Guenevere, and Sir Lancelot du Lac, the chivalrous French knight who woos her. The show would be called *Camelot* after the mythical kingdom in which bravery, truth, and justice were virtues embodied by its rulers.

The show was plagued with problems from the outset; Lerner's wife left him during the writing process, resulting in the lyricist developing a bleeding ulcer. When director Moss Hart suffered a heart attack, Lerner had to step in to replace him. (Hart would eventually die a year into the show's run.) When the show opened in Toronto, it ran nearly four hours. By the time it reached Boston (the accustomed penultimate booking before going to Broadway), the running time had been shortened substantially, but was still considered too long. At its premiere at the Majestic Theatre in New York, key songs, including the knights' threatening "Fie on Goodness" and the charming "Then You May Take Me to the Fair," had both been cut, although both have since been restored in subsequent productions.

Despite initially lukewarm reviews from critics expecting another *My Fair Lady*, *Camelot* became a huge success with the public, playing for more than two years and over 800 performances. The sumptuous costumes, glittering original cast (Richard Burton, Julie Andrews, and Robert Goulet), and one of Lerner and Loewe's most enchanting scores helped secure its status as an opulent and enduring Broadway classic.

CAMELOT

LERNER • LOEWE

CONTENTS

I WONDER WHAT THE KING IS DOING TONIGHT

Words by
ALAN JAY LERNER

Music by
FREDERICK LOEWE

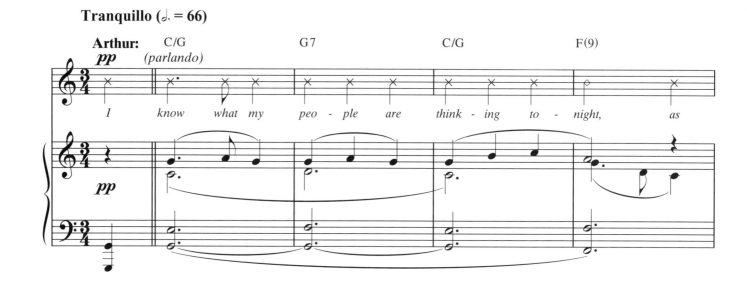

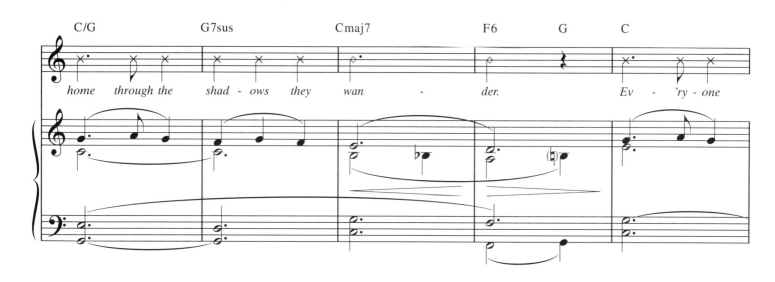

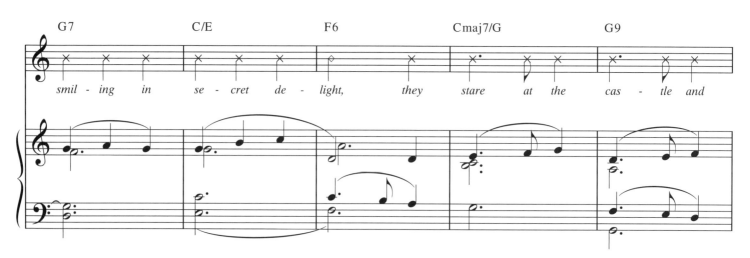

I Wonder What the King Is Doing Tonight - 8 - 1
30875

I Wonder What the King Is Doing Tonight - 8 - 2
30875

8

THE SIMPLE JOYS OF MAIDENHOOD

Words by
ALAN JAY LERNER

Music by
FREDERICK LOEWE

Shan't I, St. Genevieve? Why must I suffer this squalid destiny Just when I reach the

golden age of eligibility and wooability. Is my fate determined by love and courtship?

Oh, no. Clause one: fix the border; Clause two: establish trade;

Clause three: deliver me; Clause four: stop the war; five, six: pick up sticks. How cruel! How unjust!

Poco meno mosso

Am I never to know the joys of maidenhood? The conventional, ordinary, garden variety joys of maidenhood?

16

The Simple Joys of Maidenhood - 8 - 5
30875

CAMELOT

Words by
ALAN JAY LERNER

Music by
FREDERICK LOEWE

*Spoken or sung.

Camelot - 7 - 1
30875

21

Camelot - 7 - 2
30875

22

Camelot - 7 - 3
30875

24

Camelot - 7 - 5
30875

26

Camelot - 7 - 7
30875

FOLLOW ME

Words by
ALAN JAY LERNER

Music by
FREDERICK LOEWE

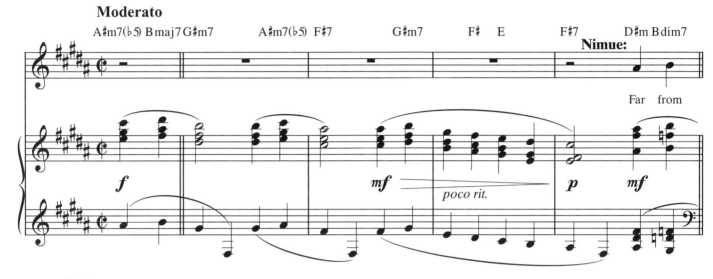

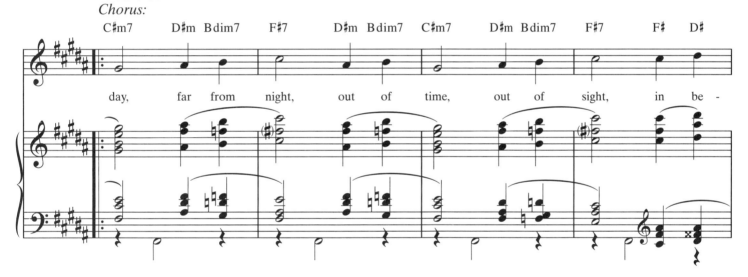

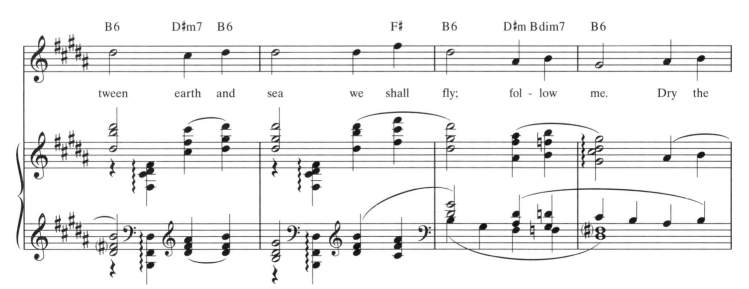

Follow Me - 3 - 1
30875

THE LUSTY MONTH OF MAY

Words by
ALAN JAY LERNER

Music by
FREDERICK LOEWE

The Lusty Month of May - 10 - 1
30875

C'EST MOI

Words by
ALAN JAY LERNER

Music by
FREDERICK LOEWE

42

THEN YOU MAY TAKE ME TO THE FAIR

Words by
ALAN JAY LERNER

Music by
FREDERICK LOEWE

Allegro con brio (♩. = 156)

Sir Lionel? Do you re-call the oth-er night that I dis-tinct-ly said you might serve as my es-cort at the next town fair?_____ Well, I'm a-fraid there's some-one who I must in-vite in place of you, some-one who

cho-sen one, I know, but it's tra-di-tion it should go to the un-

50

G/B C Cmaj7 C7 Fdim7 F Fdim7 F Am Bm/A D9 F#dim7

and young Du Lac seems strong - est, er - go, he should

($\downarrow = \downarrow .$)

C/G B/F# G7sus G7 C N.C. E

Dinadan:

take me to the cat - tle show._____ Your maj - es - ty can't be -

F/E G/B E Bm7 E Bm7 E Bm7

lieve this blus - t'ring prat - tle!_____ Let him prove it with a sword or lance in -

E N.C. G Ab/G Bb/D

stead._____ I prom - ise you when I'm done the gor - y

53

Then You May Take Me to the Fair - 11 - 8
30875

54

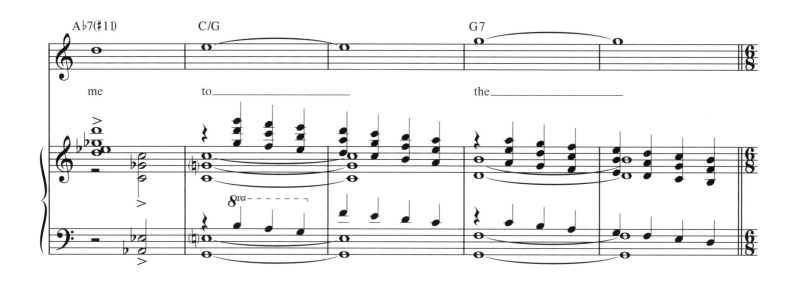

HOW TO HANDLE A WOMAN

Words by
ALAN JAY LERNER

Music by
FREDERICK LOEWE

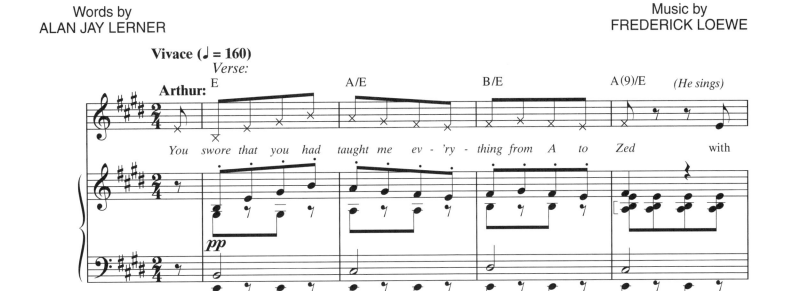

58

How to Handle a Woman - 7 - 2
30875

Moderato (♩ = 108)
Refrain:

IF EVER I WOULD LEAVE YOU

Words by
ALAN JAY LERNER

Music by
FREDERICK LOEWE

Moderato (♩ = 100)

Con espressione

Lancelot:

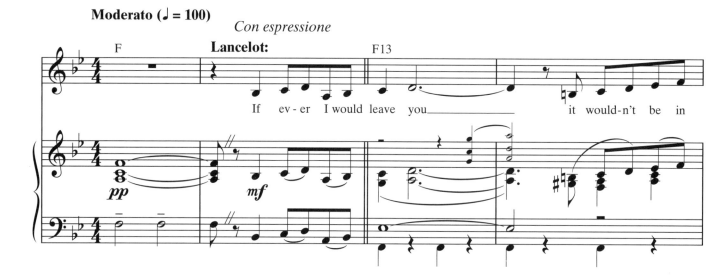

If ev-er I would leave you ____ it would-n't be in

sum - mer; ____ see-ing you in sum - mer, I nev - er would

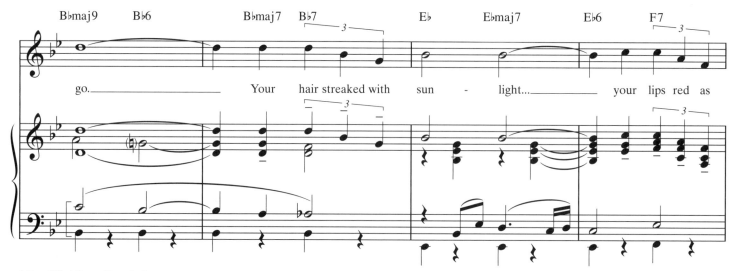

go. ____ Your hair streaked with sun - light... ____ your lips red as

If Ever I Would Leave You - 4 - 1
30875

66

If Ever I Would Leave You - 4 - 3
30875

BEFORE I GAZE AT YOU AGAIN

Words by
ALAN JAY LERNER

Music by
FREDERICK LOEWE

70

eyes a-shine like new a-gain, my man-ner poised and calm.

Stay far a-way, my love, far a-way, till

I for-get I gazed at you to-day,_____ to-

day,_____ to - day._____

Before I Gaze at You Again - 3 - 3
30875

THE SEVEN DEADLY VIRTUES

Words by
ALAN JAY LERNER

Music by
FREDERICK LOEWE

72

Lyrics:

me. Those sev-en dead-ly vir-tues, they're made for oth-er chaps who love a life of fail-ure and en-nui. Take Cour-age! Now there's a sport; an in-vi-ta-tion to the state of rig-or mort! And Pu-ri-ty; a no-ble

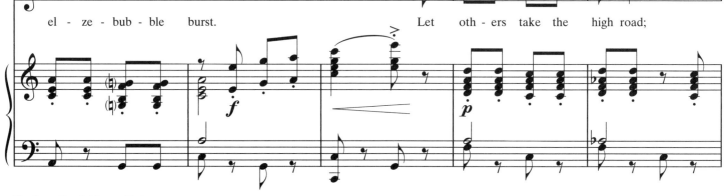

WHAT DO THE SIMPLE FOLK DO?

Words by
ALAN JAY LERNER

Music by
FREDERICK LOEWE

Moderately (♩ = 120)

What do the sim-ple folk do_____ to

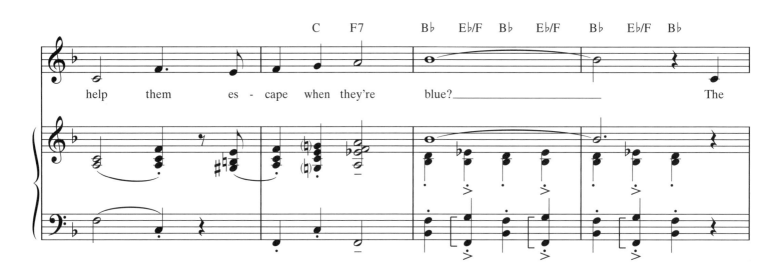

help them es-cape when they're blue?_____ The

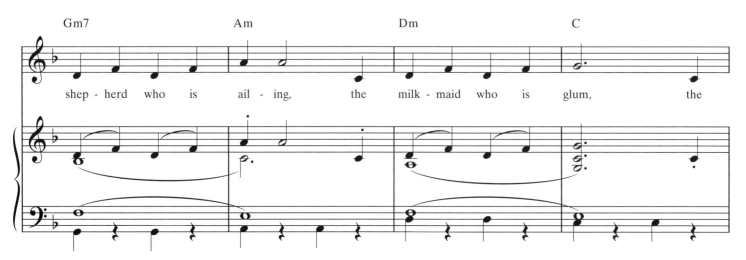

shep-herd who is ail-ing, the milk-maid who is glum, the

(Guenevere turns to him in frustration.)

world is bright, and all is right, and all is mer-ry and gay! What

Tempo I

else do the sim-ple folk do?_____ They

must have a sys-tem or two._____ They

ob-vious-ly out-shine us at turn-ing tears to mirth; have

88

What Do the Simple Folk Do? - 16 - 13
30875

What Do the Simple Folk Do? - 16 - 14
30875

90

I LOVED YOU ONCE IN SILENCE

Words by
ALAN JAY LERNER

Music by
FREDERICK LOEWE

94

I Loved You Once in Silence - 6 - 3
30875

Lancelot: Jenny, it's because we're here,
here in Camelot…
(Dialogue continues)

Optional (continuation of Scene)

Guenevere: …What sort of heartbreaking solution is that?
Lancelot: Forgive me, Jenny, *(The music begins.)*

L'istesso tempo

I shall never mention it again, I swear.

Nor shall I come to see you again. I swear that too.

Guenevere: Lance? (He stops.) Have we no more tender words to say to each

other?

(She sings)

The si - lence_____ at last was bro - ken!_____

Mordred and Knights tiptoe silently into the room.

We flung wide_____ our pris-on door._____ Ev-'ry joy-ous word of love was spo-ken... And af-ter

poco rit. *rall.*

Andante (♩ = 100)

all had been said, here we are, my love, si-lent once more and not far, my love...

colla voce

(Lancelot and Guenevere embrace.) Mordred: …Lancelot, don't touch your dagger. (Lancelot whirls around.)

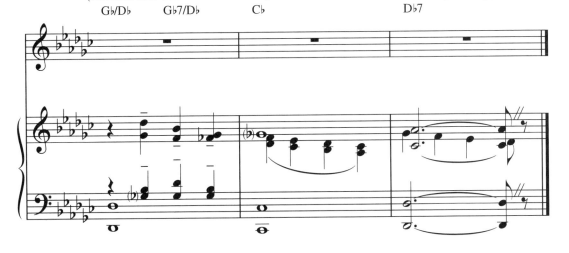

I accuse you of treason, and order you both to stand trial for your crime. Surrender in the name of the King. (Lancelot snatches the sword from Mordred.)

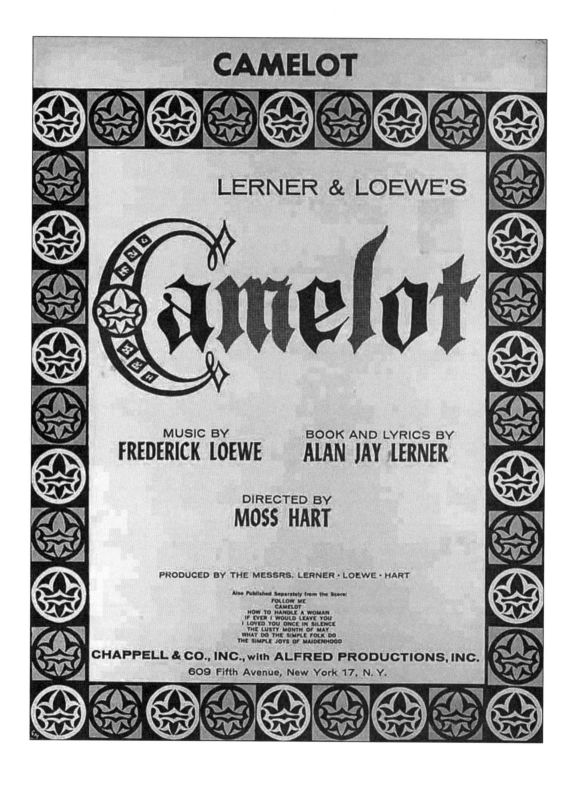

LYRICS SECTION

I WONDER WHAT THE KING IS DOING TONIGHT

Arthur: *(Spoken) I know what my people are thinking tonight,*
As home through the shadows they wander.
Ev'ryone smiling in secret delight,
They stare at the castle and ponder.

Whenever the wind blows this way,
You can almost hear ev'ryone say:
I wonder what the king is doing tonight?
What merriment is the King pursuing tonight?
The candles at the court, they never burned as bright.
I wonder what the King is up to tonight?

How goes the final hour
As he sees the bridal bower
Being legally and regally prepared?
Well, I'll tell you what the King is doing tonight:
He's scared! He's scared!

You mean that a King who fought a dragon,
Whacked him in two and fixed his wagon,
Goes to be wed in terror and distress?
(Spoken) Yes!

A warrior who's so calm in battle,
Even his armour doesn't rattle,
Faces a woman petrified with fright?
(Spoken) Right!

You mean that appalling clamoring
That sounds like a blacksmith hammering
Is merely the banging of his royal knees?
(Spoken) Please!

You wonder what the King is wishing tonight.
He's wishing he were in Scotland, fishing tonight.
What occupies his time while waiting for his bride?
He's searching high and low for some place to hide,

And oh, the expectation,
The sublime anticipation
He must feel about the wedding night to come!

(Spoken) Well! (Sung) I'll tell you what the King is feeling tonight:
He's numb! He shakes!
He quails! He quakes!
And that's what the King is doing tonight!

THE SIMPLE JOYS OF MAIDENHOOD

Guenevere: St. Genevieve! St. Genevieve!
It's Guenevere! Remember me?
St. Genevieve! St. Genevieve!
I'm over here beneath this tree.
You know how faithful and devout I am.
You must admit I've always been a lamb.

But Genevieve, St. Genevieve,
I won't obey you anymore!
You've gone a bit too far.
I won't be bid and bargain'd for
Like beads at a bazaar.

St. Genevieve, I've run away,
Eluded them and fled,
And from now on I intend to pray
To someone else instead.

Oh, Genevieve, St. Genevieve,
Where were you when my youth was sold?
Dear Genevieve, sweet Genevieve,
Shan't I be young before I'm old?

(Spoken) Shan't I, St. Genevieve? Why must I suffer this squalid destiny
Just when I reach the golden age of eligibility and wooability.
Is my fate determined by love and courtship?
Oh, no. Clause one: fix the border; Clause two: establish trade;
Clause three: deliver me; Clause four: stop the war; five, six: pick up sticks.
How cruel! How unjust! Am I never to know the joys of maidenhood?
The conventional, ordinary, garden variety joys of maidenhood?

(Sung) Where are the simple joys of maidenhood?
Where are all those adoring, daring boys?
Where's the knight pining so for me?
He leaps to death in woe for me.
Oh, where are a maiden's simple joys?

Shan't I have the normal life a maiden should?
Shall I never be rescued in the wood?
Shall two knights never tilt for me
And let their blood be spilt for me?
Oh, where are the simple joys of maidenhood?

Shall I not be on a pedestal,
Worshipped and competed for;
Not be carried off, or better st'll,
Cause a little war?

Where are the simple joys of maidenhood?
Are these sweet, gentle pleasures gone for good?
Shall a feud not begin for me?
Shall kith not kill their kin for me?
Oh, where are the trivial joys?
Harmless, convivial joys?
Where are the simple joys of maidenhood?

CAMELOT

Arthur: *(Spoken) It's true! It's true!*
The crown has made it clear:
The climate must be perfect
(Sung) All the year.

A law was made a distant moon ago here:
July and August cannot be too hot.
And there's a legal limit to the snow here
In Camelot.

The winter is forbidden till December
And exits March the second on the dot.
By order, summer lingers through September
In Camelot.

Camelot! Camelot!
I know it sounds a bit bizarre,
But in Camelot, Camelot,
That's how conditions are.

The rain may never fall till after sundown.
By eight, the morning fog must disappear.
In short, there's simply not
A more congenial spot
For happ'ly ever-aftering
Than here in Camelot!

Guenevere: *(Spoken) And I suppose the autumn leaves fall in neat little piles.*
Arthur: *Oh, no, Milady, they blow away completely. At night, of course.*
Guenevere: *Of course!*

Arthur: *(Sung)* Camelot! Camelot!
I know it gives a person pause,
But in Camelot! Camelot!
Those are the legal laws.

The snow may never slush upon the hillside.
By 9 p.m. the moonlight must appear.
In short, there's simply not
A more congenial spot
For happ'ly ever-aftering
Than here in Camelot.

FOLLOW ME

Nimue: Far from day, far from night,
Out of time, out of sight,
In between, earth and sea
We shall fly; follow me.

Dry the rain, warm the snow;
Where the winds never go
Follow me, follow me, follow me.

To a cave by a sapphire shore,
Where we'll walk through an emerald door
And for thousands of breathless evermores
My life you shall be.

Only you, only I,
World farewell, world goodbye.
To our home 'neath the sea
We shall fly; follow me.
Follow me, follow me, follow me.

THE LUSTY MONTH OF MAY

Guenevere: Tra la! It's May!
The lusty month of May!
That lovely month when ev'ryone goes
Blissfully astray.
Tra la! It's here!
That shocking time of year!
When tons of wicked little thoughts
Merrily appear.

It's May! It's May!
That gorgeous holiday,
When ev'ry maiden
Prays that her lad
Will be a cad!

It's mad! It's gay!
A libelous display.
Those dreary vows that ev'ryone takes,
Ev'ryone breaks,
Ev'ryone makes divine mistakes.
The lusty month of May!

Whence this fragrance wafting through the air?
What sweet feelings does its scent transmute?
Whence this perfume floating ev'rywhere?
Don't you know it's that dear forbidden fruit?

Tra la la la la! That dear forbidden fruit.
Tra la la la la!
Tra la la la la!
Tra la!
Tra la!
Tra la la la la la la la la la.

It's May! The lusty month of May!
That darling month when ev'ryone throws
Self control away.
It's time to do
A wretched thing or two,
And try to make each precious day
One you'll always rue.

It's May! It's May!
The month of "Yes, you may."
The time for ev'ry frivolous whim,
Proper or "im."

It's wild, it's gay
A blot in ev'ry way.
The birds, the bees with all of their vast
Amorous past
Gaze at the human race aghast.
Chorus: The lusty month of May!

Guenevere: Tra la! It's May!
The lusty month of May!
Chorus: That lovely month when ev'ryone goes
Blissfully astray.

Tra la! It's here!
That shocking time of year
When tons of wicked little thoughts
Merrily appear.

It's May! It's May!
The month of great dismay,
Guenevere: When all the world is
Brimming with fun,
Wholesome or "un."

It's mad! It's gay!
A libelous display.
Those dreary vows that ev'ryone takes,
Ev'ryone breaks.
Ev'ryone makes divine mistakes.
The lusty month of May!

C'EST MOI

Lancelot: Camelot! Camelot!
In far off France I heard your call.
Camelot! Camelot!
And here am I to give my all.

I know in my soul what you expect of me,
And all that and more I shall be!
A knight of the table round should be invincible,
Succeed where a less fantastic man would fail.
Climb a wall no one else can climb,
Cleave a dragon in record time,
Swim a moat in a coat of heavy iron mail.

No matter the pain, he ought to be unwinceable;
Impossible deeds should be his daily fare.
But where in the world is there in the world
A man so extr'ordinaire?

C'est moi! C'est moi! I'm forced to admit!
'Tis I, I humbly reply.
That mortal who these marvels can do,
C'est moi, c'est moi, 'tis I!

I've never lost in battle or game.
I'm simply the best by far.
When swords are crossed, 'tis always the same:
One blow and au revoir!

C'est moi! C'est moi! So admir'bly fit,
A French Prometheus unbound.
And here I stand with valor untold,
Exception'lly brave, amazingly bold,
To serve at the table round!

The soul of a knight should be a thing remarkable;
His heart and his mind as pure as morning dew.
With a will and a self restraint
That's the envy of ev'ry saint,
He could easily work a miracle or two!

To love and desire, he ought to be unsparkable;
The ways of the flesh should offer no allure.
But where in the world
Is there in the world
A man so untouched and pure?

C'est moi! C'est moi! I blush to disclose,
I'm far too noble to lie.
That man in whom
These qualities bloom,
C'est moi, c'est moi, 'tis I!

I've never strayed from all I believe.
I'm blessed with an iron will.
Had I been made the partner of Eve,
We'd be in Eden still.

C'est moi! C'est moi! The angels have chose
To fight their battles below.
And here I stand as pure as a prayer,
Incredibly clean, with virtue to spare,
The godliest man I know
C'est moi!

THEN YOU MAY TAKE ME TO THE FAIR

Guenevere: *(Spoken) Sir Lionel?*
(Sung) Do you recall the other night
That I distinctly said you might
Serve as my escort at the next town fair?

Well, I'm afraid there's someone who
I must invite in place of you,
Someone who plainly is beyond compare.
That Frenchman's pow'r is more tremendous
Than I have e'er seen anywhere,
And when a man is that stupendous,
He by right should take me to the fair.

Sir Lionel: Your majesty, let me tilt with him and smite him.
Don't refuse me so abruptly, I implore.
Oh, give me the opportunity to fight him,
And Gaul will be divided once more.

Guenevere: *(Spoken) You will bash and thrash him?*
Sir Lionel: *(Spoken) I'll smash and mash him!*
Guenevere: *(Spoken) You'll give him trouble?*
Sir Lionel: *(Spoken) He will be rubble!*
Guenevere: *(Spoken) A mighty whack!*
Sir Lionel: *(Spoken) His skull will crack!*

Guenevere: *(Spoken) Well!*
(Sung) Then you may take me to the fair,
If you do all the things you promise.
In fact, my heart will break
Should you not take me to the fair.

(Spoken) Sir Sagramore?
(Sung) I have some rather painful news
Relative to the subject who's
To be beside me at the next court ball.
You were the chosen one I know,
But it's tradition it should go
To the unquestioned champion in the hall.

And I'm convinced that splendid Frenchman
Can eas'ly conquer one and all,
And besting all our local henchmen,
He should sit beside me at the ball.

Sir Sagramore: I beg of you, ma'am, withhold your invitation;
I swear to you this challenge will be met.
And when I have finished up the operation,
I'll serve him to Your Highness en brochette!

Guenevere: *(Spoken) You'll pierce right through him?*
Sir Sagramore: *(Spoken) I'll barbecue him!*
Guenevere: *(Spoken) A wicked thrust!*
Sir Sagramore: *(Spoken) 'Twill be dust to dust!*
Guenevere: *(Spoken) From fore to aft?*
Sir Sagramore: *(Spoken) He'll feel a draft!*

Guenevere: *(Spoken) Well, then...*
(Sung) You may sit by me at the ball
If you demolish him in battle.
In fact, I know I'd cry
Were you not by me at the ball.

(Spoken) Sir Dinadan?
(Sung) Didn't I promise that you may
Guide me to London on the day
That I go up to judge the cattle show?
As it is quite a nasty ride,
There must be someone at my side
Who'll be defending me from beast and foe.

So when I choose whom I prefer go,
I take the strongest knight I know,
And young Du Lac seems strongest, ergo,
He should take me to the cattle show.

Sir Dinadan: Your majesty can't believe this blust'ring prattle!
Let him prove it with a sword or lance instead.
I promise you when I'm done this gory battle,
His shoulders will be lonesome for his head!

Guenevere: *(Spoken) You'll disconnect him?*
Sir Dinadan: *(Spoken) I'll vivisect him!*
Guenevere: *(Spoken) You'll open wide him?*
Sir Dianadan: *(Spoken) I'll subdivide him!*
Guenevere: *(Spoken) Oh, dear, dear, dear, dear, dear!*

(Sung) Then you may guide me to the show,
If you can carry out your programme.
In fact, I'd grieve inside
Should you not guide me to the show.

Knights: Milady, we shall put an end to
That Gallic bag of noise and nerve.
When we do all that we intend to,
He'll be a plate of French hors d'oeuvres!

Guenevere: I do applaud your noble goals;
Now let us see if you achieve them.
And if you do, then you will
Be the three who will go
To the ball, to the show,
And take me to the fair!

HOW TO HANDLE A WOMAN

Arthur: *(Spoken) You swore that you had taught me*
Ev'rything from A to Zed,
(Sung) With nary an omission in between.
Well, I shall tell you what you obviously forgot:
That's how a ruler rules a queen!

And what of teaching me
By turning me to animal and bird,
From beaver to the smallest bobolink!
I should have had a whirl
At changing to a girl,
To learn the way the creatures think!

But wasn't there a night, on a summer long gone by,
We pass'd a couple wrangling away;
And did I not say, "Merlyn, what if that chap were I?"
And did he not give counsel and say…
"What was it now? My mind's a wall.
Oh, yes! By Jove, now I recall:"

"How to handle a woman,
There's a way," said the wise old man.
"A way known by ev'ry woman
Since the whole rig'marole began."

"Do I flatter her?" I begged him answer.
"Do I threaten or cajole or plead?
Do I brood or play the gay romancer?"
Said he, smiling, "No indeed."

"How to handle a woman?
Mark me well, I will tell you, sir.
The way to handle a woman is to love her,
Simply love her,
Merely love her,
Love her,
Love her."

108

IF EVER I WOULD LEAVE YOU

Lancelot: If ever I would leave you,
It wouldn't be in summer.
Seeing you in summer,
I never would go.

Your hair streaked with sunlight,
Your lips red as flame,
Your face with a lustre,
That puts gold to shame.

But if I'd ever leave you,
How could it be in autumn?
How I'd leave in autumn,
I never would know.

I've seen how you sparkle
When fall nips the air.
I know you in autumn
And I must be there.

And could I leave you running merrily through the snow
Or on a wintry evening when you catch the fire's glow?

If ever I would leave you,
How could it be in springtime,
Knowing how in spring I'm
Bewitch'd by you so?

Oh, no, not in springtime!
Summer, winter or fall!
No, never could I leave you
At all!

BEFORE I GAZE AT YOU AGAIN

Guenevere: Before I gaze at you again,
I'll need a time for tears.
Before I gaze at you again,
Let hours turn to years.

I have so much forgetting to do
Before I try to gaze again at you.

Stay away until you cross my mind
Barely once a day,
Till the moment I awake and find
I can smile and say

That I can gaze at you again
Without a blush or qualm,
My eyes a-shine like new again,
My manner poised and calm.

Stay far away,
My love, far away.
Till I forget I gazed at you today,
Today, today.

THE SEVEN DEADLY VIRTUES

Mordred: The seven deadly virtues,
Those ghastly little traps,
Oh no, Milord, they weren't meant for me.

Those seven deadly virtues
They're made for other chaps
Who love a life of failure and ennui.

Take Courage! Now there's a sport;
An invitation to the state of rigor mort!
And Purity, a noble yen,
And very restful ev'ry now and then.

I find Humility means to be hurt.
It's not the earth the meek inherit, it's the dirt.
Honesty is fatal. It should be taboo.
Diligence, a fate I would hate.

If Charity means giving, I give it to you,
And Fidelity is only for your mate. Hah!
You'll never find a virtue unstatusing my quo,
Or making my Beelze-bubble burst.

Let others take the high road; I will take the low.
I cannot wait to rush in where angels fear to go.
With all those seven deadly virtues,
Free and happy little me has not been cursed!

WHAT DO THE SIMPLE FOLK DO?

Guenevere: What do the simple folk do
To help them escape when they're blue?
The shepherd who is ailing, the milkmaid who is glum,
The cobbler who is wailing from nailing his thumb?
When they're beset and besieged,
The folk not nobless'ly obliged,
However do they manage to shed their weary lot?
Oh, what do simple folk do, we do not?

Arthur: I have been informed by those who know them well,
They find relief in quite a clever way.
When they're sorely pressed, they whistle for a spell,
And whistling seems to brighten up their day.
And that's what simple folk do, so they say.

Guenevere: *(Spoken) They whistle?*

Arthur: *(Spoken) So they say.*

Guenevere: *(Sung)* What else do the simple folk do
To perk up the heart and get through?
The wee folk and the grown folk who wander to and fro
Have ways known to their own folk we throne folk don't know.
When all the doldrums begin,
What keeps each of them in his skin?
What ancient native custom provides the needed glow?
Oh, what do simple folk do? Do you know?

Arthur: Once along the road I came upon a lad
Singing in a voice three times his size.
When I asked him why, he told me he was sad,
And singing always made his spirits rise.
And that's what simple folk do, I surmise.

Guenevere: *(Spoken) They… sing.*
Arthur: *(Spoken) I surmise.*

Together: *(Sung)* Arise, my love! Arise, my love!
Apollo's lighting the skies, my love.
The meadows shine with columbine and daffodils blossom away.
Hear Venus call to one and all: "Come taste delight while you may.
The world is bright and all is right and life is merry and gay!"

Guenevere: What else do the simple folk do?
They must have a system or two.
They obviously outshine us at turning tears to mirth;
Have tricks a royal highness is minus from birth.
What then, I wonder do they
To chase all the goblins away?
They have some tribal sorc'ry you haven't mentioned yet.
Oh, what do simple folk do to forget?

Arthur: Often I am told they dance a fiery dance,
And whirl 'til they're completely uncontrolled.
Soon the mind is blank and all are in a trance,
A vi'lent trance astounding to behold.
And that's what simple folk do, so I'm told.

Guenevere: What else do the simple folk do
To help them escape when they're blue?

Arthur: They sit around and wonder what royal folk would do,
And that's what simple folk do.

Guenevere: *(Spoken) Oh, no, really?*
Arthur: *(Spoken) I have it on the best authority.*

Together: *(Sung)* Yes, that's what simple folk do.

I LOVED YOU ONCE IN SILENCE

Guenevere: I loved you once in silence
And mis'ry was all I knew.
Trying so to keep my love from showing,
All the while not knowing you loved me too.

Yes, loved me in lonesome silence;
Your heart filled with dark despair.
Thinking love would flame in you forever,
And I'd never, never know the flame was there.

Then one day we cast away our secret longing;
The raging tide we held inside would hold no more.
The silence at last was broken.
We flung wide our prison door.
Ev'ry joyous word of love was spoken,
And now there's twice as much grief, twice the strain for us,
Twice the despair, twice the pain for us
As we had known before.

The silence at last was broken;
We flung wide our prison door.
Ev'ry joyous word of love was spoken,
And after all had been said,
Here we are, my love,
Silent once more
And not far, my love
From where we were before.

CAMELOT (reprise)

Arthur: Each evening, from December to December,
Before you drift to sleep upon your cot,
Think back on all the tales that you'll remember
Of Camelot.

Ask every person if he's heard the story;
And tell it strong and clear if he has not,
That once there was a fleeting wisp of glory
Called Camelot.

Chorus: Camelot! Camelot!
I know it gives a person pause.
But in Camelot, Camelot,
Those were the legal laws.

Arthur: Where once it never rained till after sundown,
By 8 a.m. the morning fog had flown.
Don't let it be forgot
That once there was a spot,
For one brief shining moment
That was known as Camelot.

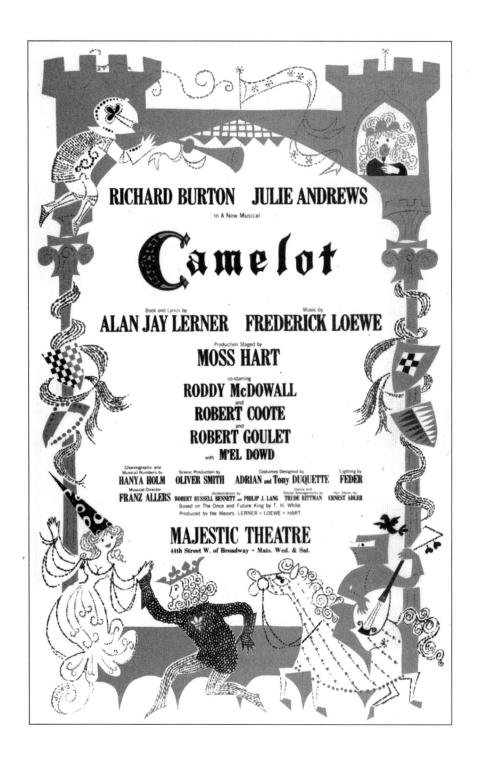